The Ramblings
of a Sussex Poet

by
Jonathan Bryant

Published by:
Brigantes Publishing – Sussex
The Laurels
30 Archibald Road
Worthing
West Sussex
BN11 2SL
01903 823258

First published in 2014
ISBN – 0-9541788-3-1

Printed by:
BPUK, Remus House, Coltsfoot Drive,
Woodston, Peterborough PE2 9BF

Contents

6   Devil's Dyke
7   Illustration
8   The Changing Of The Games
9   Wild About Harry
10 Memories Of Sussex
11 Ode To The Skylark
12 Soap
13 Kippers Galore
    Mole in a Hole
    Spring In The Bloomers
14 Brothers
15 Illustration
16 A Fleeting Meeting
17 Happiness
18 A Million Diamonds
19 Worthing Air Show
20 The Nifty Fifties
22 Fifties Brighton
23 Hove
24 Pillow Talk
    Come Fishing
25 Illustration
26 Daydreams Of Worthing
27 Cissbury Ring
28 The West Pier
29 Evening Foxtrot

30   The Kingfisher
31   The Lizard
32   Success
        Peace
33   A Sense Of Paradise
34   Dream-Cloud
35   Champion Of Cheerfulness
36   Crazy Logic
37   Illustration
38   Elders Of The Chapel
39   Mutton-Glutton
40   The Lady On The Bike
41   Illustration
42   Sign Of The Times
43   Birth Of Romance
44   The Old Wurthytrudger
45   The Lurgashall Venture
46   Sweetie
47   The Missing Tarts
49   Flashy Fellow
50   The Brighton Line

Introduction

The first meaning for 'rambling' in Chambers Dictionary is 'walking for pleasure'. An alternative word found in the thesaurus is 'wandering'. Ever since childhood my family have loved rambling and wandering in the countryside.

Now my ramblings are more in the literary sense; not only do I wander through my memory banks, sifting and searching, I also rely on imagination coupled with occasional eureka moments. A combination of these elements have resulted in 'The Ramblings Of A Sussex Poet'.

Please feel free to join me.

Devil's Dyke

When I was young we used to hike
From Brighton to the Devil's Dyke
In those days we would get our thrills
From roly-polys down the hills.
I remember that old cosy shack
Where ramblers used to buy a snack
But with the passing of the days
We see a changing of the ways.

Now hordes of people think it swell
To party at the Dyke Hotel
They're rushing to the great outdoors
In camper vans and four-by-fours
And dogs and children by the scores
Ramblers, riders and hang-gliders
Joggers, hikers, hairy bikers
Rush to join the 'Devil's Dykers'.

Then when the day is nearly done
We watch the setting of the sun
With cameras clicking one by one
And people – people having fun.

The Changing Of The Games

I remember when as just a lad
The very many games we had
Four boys, two girls and Mum and Dad –
Seated round our table.

In those days we weren't into judo
We played chess and draughts and ludo
Monopoly or even Cluedo –
Seated round our table.

The evenings when the lights were low
We'd listen to a radio show
'Take It From Here' or 'Have A Go' –
Seated round our table.

It was my mother's wartime boast
We always had our Sunday roast
That was the meal we all liked most –
Seated round our table.

But nowadays the games have changed
The kids are getting quite deranged
And party times are not arranged –
Now Father's sold the table.

So all the children love to play
Computer games the livelong day
Then eat their dinner on a tray –
Seated round our telly.

Wild About Harry

I am a cat called Harry
Just like Harry Potter
My mistress has deserted me
I think she is a rotter.

This fellow comes to feed me
I think he's rather queer
He doesn't pat me on the head
Nor even scratch my ear.

My mis. is in the south of France
Sunbathing by a river
And though I'm feeling fed up now
I'll be a good forgiver.

Because she is my everything
Provider, nurse and friend
I know within my furry heart
She'll love me to the end.

Memories Of Sussex

I lay upon the grass at Beachy Head
The vista seemed to stretch beyond the skies
A feather-light, cool breeze caressed my face
As memories were stirred by seagulls' cries.

I remember, as a boy, that Barcombe Mills
Was but a sixpenny steam-train ride away
We'd sit till evening fishing in the Ouse
Till twilight came to gild the perfect day.

That sunny day I spent at Falmer pond
The water birds were fussing in the reeds
I left my two pound jam-jar on the bank
But the canny newts were hiding in the weeds.

Whilst dropping into Arundel one day
The flood plain was a picture to espy
A flight of geese were travelling through the frame
To a backdrop of the castle up on high.

The Wetlands welcome visitors year round
Where feathered friends can satisfy their needs
And buzzards soar on high above the lake
And Ratty puffs and paddles through the reeds.

I walked the Ring and breezes fanned my hair
The skylark trilled on high its melody
And as I strolled around that well-worn path
I saw an island rising from the sea.

I stood beside the Adur as day dawned
And surveyed the waters, swollen by the tide
As a mist rose from the meadows round about
And herons fished the river side by side.

I sat upon the rocks at evening's glow
As the sun sank like a furnace in the sea
And heard the waves come crashing on the shore
And thought, my Maker has been good to me.

Ode To The Skylark

Ah, little feathered songster
So precious!
How I thrill to your joyous melody.
Hanging in space
The sky is your stage
The High Down is your theatre.
Ever eager to sing
To whoever will listen.
Where did you learn such composition?
By law, inspired to perform
Your celestial symphony
So pleasing to humanity
And me – and free!

Soap

I lost the soap in the bath one day
Like a will-o'-the-wisp it slithered away
I tried to snatch it like catching a fish
'Oh! Slippery rascal, get back in the dish.'

Hither and thither my fingers did grope
How could it evade me? That small bar of soap
I stirred up the water and saw it flash by
But some of the mixture got into my eye.

It slithered around and it tickled my toes
I snorted and snuffled with soap up my nose
It eluded my grasp like an eel in a pond
Before and behind and below and beyond.

My temper was going and panic set in
I thrashed and I splashed with a terrible din
The slippery customer wanted a fight
The soap, it was laughing and still out of sight.

But then like a fool like a lamb to the slaughter
I made a mistake and stood up in the water
Like a missile I rocketed out of the bath
Straight through the window and onto the path.

The force of the impact provoked a great shout
Curtains were parted and neighbours looked out
I lay in the garden and felt such a dope
Defeated and shamed by a small bar of soap.

Kippers Galore

Today, while in my carpet slippers
I scoffed a dozen pairs of kippers
And then I wandered in the park
And thought I heard a kipper bark
But then – my goodness! Gracious me!
I saw a kipper up a tree
So now I find I can't unwind
Those kippers tangle with my mind
So folks, when you are feeling chipper
Resist – refuse that second kipper
Just do not overdose yourself
But leave the kippers on the shelf.

Mole In A Hole

A workman exclaimed 'Bless my soul!'
When he fell in a newly dug hole
There wasn't much room
As he sat in the gloom
Whilst explored by a curious mole.

Spring In The Bloomers

The celebrities took to the floor
And danced to a musical score
Then a plucky old biddy
Twirled round and got giddy
So her bloomers received an encore.

Brothers

When we were young we used to roam
The Roman Camp and far beyond
Then ambled up the Lewes Road
To catch the newts in Falmer pond.

We scampered through the farmer's fields
Avoiding all the cattle cakes
And made our way to Patcham Downs
To search for lizards and for snakes.

We strode the winding, dusty road
As we set off for Ditchling Beacon
With Marmite rolls and ginger pop
Provisions, so we wouldn't weaken.

Oh! How I loved those carefree days
When we could walk, it seemed, forever
How time enhances memories
Could I forget them? Ever. – Never!

A Fleeting Meeting

This is a secret,
Up till now, that I have kept.
Last night I went to sleep
And while slept
I was transported
And my spirit leaped.

How could it happen?
However could this be?
For there you were
In Paradise with me.

We wandered in a meadow
Near a stream
I pinched myself and asked
'Is this a dream?'

But no! – we splashed barefoot
I felt the water, cool
Then hugged you
As we rested by a pool.

I smelled your perfume –
You were really there
You smiled and ran your fingers
Through my hair.

And just as joy transcended –
It ended.

I woke with feelings
That I can't explain.
Perhaps tomorrow night
We'll meet again.

Happiness

Some people can feel very happy
With a new car that sits in the drive
And others can be quite contented
With the pleasure of being alive.

Still others are getting excitement
From a family trip to the zoo
And some will derive satisfaction
With a stairlift to get to the loo.

For joy is a state you can't measure
It surely is all in the mind
The things that bring some people pleasure
By others are swiftly declined.

If winning the pools makes you happy
And you laugh, for you don't have a care
I'll not be a teeny bit jealous
As long as you give me a share.

A Million Diamonds

A million diamonds danced upon the sea
The sky was inky black, the moon was high
Shedding its silver light upon the waves –
We stood entranced and marvelled, You and I.

A ribbon of jewels twinkled on the coast
Adorning hamlets nestling in the bays
The night birds wheeled and dived on silent wings
Reminding me of treasured happy days.

And so I reminisced beside the shore –
That diamond ring I purchased, all in vain
The evening sparked so many memories –
What would I give to see your face again.

But I still see you with my inward eye
For life was briefly kind to you and me
I won't forget the magic when, that night,
A million diamonds danced upon the sea.

Worthing Air Show

See the gulls gliding over the glistening waters
Their bright eyes alert as down they dart
Their eager beaks pierce the surface
As they seek sustenance from the ocean's pantry.
Others scavenge the seashore
Searching for scraps and morsels
As fishermen prepare their catch.

Overhead a gang of gulls pursue one of their
Fellows as he retreats with his trophy.
Attracted by the rumpus the crows, ever alert,
Join the melee – food is forgotten as old rivals
Engage in aerial combat.

Screaming, crying, feathers flying
More arriving, wheeling, diving.
Then – as if by bugle's call
An ending to the free for all.

The seagulls resume ocean patrol
The crows return to the shore, peace is restored.

Watching from the pier
I am fascinated by life's theatre.

The Nifty Fifties

When you reach fifty
And can't touch your toes
You're rapidly growing
Out of your clothes.
Forget those lunches
At the local pub
And go and join the
Phoenix Club.

There's sports, gymnastics
And yoga as well
But the dancing is funky
Why not join for a spell?

Slow, slow, quick, quick
Foxtrot, waltz
Hit the floor
And feel the force.

Dancing the waltz
They say is a doddle
But as we get tired
We tend to waddle.
We start to tango
With knees well bent
But our knees drop lower
Until we are spent,

Carol is ruling
So no one can skive
The music is crazy
As we jump and jive.

People who spy us
Go ha, ha, ha
When they see us learning
The cha, cha, cha.
Next we sample
A groovy number
As we attempt
To dance the rumba.

When we're worn out
And ready for sleep
We can only manage
To do the creep.

So if you want to have fun
And roll out the barrel
Go and sign up
For lessons with Carol.

This poem is based on experiences with the over fifties club at the Durrington Leisure Centre.

Fifties Brighton

Ah – those were the days, in the fifties
When Brighton was host to all sorts
There were tinkers and tailors and soldiers
And sailors from various ports.

When boys and girls danced at the Regent
With a shimmering sphere up above
And the floor was alive with the power
Of music and jiving and love.

The coffee shops sprouted all over
Where the glittering jukebox was king
And people would part with their sixpence
Just to hear all their favourites sing.

The West Pier rejoiced in its glory
A feat of Victorian art
Before it was claimed by the starlings
And negligence ripped out its heart.

Folk would visit Blackrock in the morning
And play in the pools by the sea
Catch winkles and shrimps by the dozen
And then take them home for their tea.

There were tigers in Brighton in those days
You could see them perform for a price
And after they'd mauled their opponents
We were all free to take to the ice.

And every new year from the station
A message was heard, loud and clear
From the steam trains all sounding their whistles
To herald the start of the year.

Though Brighton has changed through the ages
The Palace Pier still reigns supreme
Where you get a grand view of the coastline
Or sit in the sun and just dream.

Hove

When I was young I used to rove
Along the avenues of Hove
Then through the Lanes of Brighton, too
And down the pier to see the view.

When people ask where I come from
I say, whilst strolling on the prom
'I come from Brighton by the sea,
Well that's not quite true, Hove actually.'

Pillow Talk

Another day of feeling ill
I think I'll take another pill
And then go up the wooden hill
To bed.

Another night of sleep and rest
I think I have regained my zest
The magic pillow has de-stressed
My head.

So now I face another day
The blackbird sings a roundelay
And all my feelings of dismay
Have fled.

Come Fishing

When the family went to Capri
We excitedly bathed in the sea
As Grandad's costume
Had plenty of room
He caught us some fish for our tea.

Daydreams Of Worthing

When you arrive at Worthing
Just sit there, on the pier
And look along the coastline –
A view that's bound to cheer.

You'll see the Seven Sisters
That host the coastal walk
Become a waving ribbon
As the sun lights up the chalk.

And if your eyes are focussed,
And if the weather's right,
And if the mist has lifted
You might see the Isle of Wight.

Then once a year the Waverley,
A ship from days of steam,
Sets off on her nostalgic trip
For those who like to dream.

To Eastbourne via Beachy Head
Just cruising at your leisure
Returning in the evening light
With memories to treasure.

Cissbury Ring

One day I looked to Cissbury Ring
And saw her smiling face
It seemed she was inviting me
To feel her fond embrace.

I ambled up the gentle path
That led me through the trees
The trees were all a'murmuring
Responding to the breeze.

Then when I reached the ancient ring
That overlooks the sea
The skylarks with their joyful song
Rose up to welcome me.

Just as an eagle on the heights
Surveys his chosen land
I felt a sense of freedom
From the countryside I scanned.

The Seven Sisters in the sun
Enjoyed the evening light –
Contrasting with the Sussex Weald –
A switchback gleaming white.

And looking west expectantly
Across the hills of baize
I glimpsed the bashful Isle of Wight
Veiled by a summer haze.

So if you're feeling down at heart
Then please take this advice
Go rest awhile on Cissbury Ring
And sample Paradise.

The West Pier

Ah! Those treasured memories
Of leisure days in a bygone age
Fishing from your landing stage
Watching the Waverley riding the waves.

A human kaleidoscope covered your deck
Sailors from faraway ports
Girls in shorts, beads around necks
Lip gloss, candyfloss
Gaming machines
Children chewing jelly beans.
Deckchairs with fat ladies
Enjoying the breeze
Grandad with trousers
Rolled up to the knees
Soaking up sun, no hat on his head
A hanky instead.

Now you stand – a blackened hulk
Rising defiantly out of the sea
Long may we grieve –
Even the starlings have taken their leave.

Evening Foxtrot

I saw him by the Adur
With a rabbit in his jaws
His red tail proud and bushy
As he loped without a pause.

His eyes were two green almonds
His head erect with pride
As he carried home his trophy
By the misty riverside.

Through rushes by the river
He made a graceful leap
His lifeless bundle swaying
As he neared a flock of sheep.

He didn't seem to worry
When he saw me by the stile
Although he kept his distance –
And I swear I saw him smile.

Then he seemed to vanish
In the long grass, hid from men
Was a hungry vixen waiting?
With her fox cubs in the den.

The Kingfisher

Just by the stream in Brooklands Park
One sunny April day
I had a sweet experience
That took my breath away.

I saw an iridescent flash
Of light before my eyes
And glimpsed a swiftly moving bird
Diminutive in size.

I longed to see it once again
As I sat by the stream
Could I have just been dozing off?
And was it just a dream?

I hid behind the willow tree
And peered across the reeds
I scanned the water, up and down,
Just where the minnow feeds.

I heard a splash and looked round
Then satisfied my wish
For 'neath the surface seemed to be
A little feathered fish.

It rose up from the river-bed
On wings that beat so fast
A small fish glistened in its beak
As it went flying past.

Once more I viewed its brilliance
Perched there upon a tree
I feel I have been privileged
To share this memory.

The Lizard

I spied him in a grassy hide
Drawn by his beady little eyes
And movement, quick, from side to side
Relentlessly he stalked his prize
The fattest of a group of flies.
The fly was basking in the dust
The lizard made a rapier thrust
With lightning speed he snapped her up
To satisfy his hunger lust
Then rested in the sun to sup.

Success

Sweet is the sleep of the servant
Who gathers not riches nor fame
He covets no other man's woman
And treats all his fellows the same.

Sweet is the sleep of the person
Who does not experience shame
When those all around him are cheating
His conscience absolves him from blame.

Sweet is the sleep of the fellow
Who values the sick and the lame
He seeks no esteem or approval
His reward is to have a good name.

Peace?

I remember the joy
As a boy
When I heard the bells ring
And Vera Lynn sing
To signal war's end
When peace would transcend –

What happened?

A Sense Of Paradise

When I taste the first strawberries of summer
And sip a Pimms on the lawn
I remember Gran's shrimp teas –
And think of paradise.

When I hear the wind in the trees
The waves lapping the seashore
The cheerful song of the blackbird –
I long for paradise.

When I see a wood full of bluebells
A field of ripe wheat and poppies
Spring lambs gaily gambolling –
I'm close to paradise.

When I recall the smell of a wood fire
The heady fragrance of honeysuckle
The perfume of my beloved –
I yearn for paradise.

When I feel the breeze in my hair
The essence of a summer day
The gentle touch of a dear one –
I'm in Paradise!

Dream-Cloud

An angel surveyed a rainbow
That had survived a rainstorm.
The angel exclaimed 'How beautiful!
What a shame to lose you.'

The red was a field of poppies
On a hot summer's day.
Orange brought to mind
Arrangements of mellow fruits
Of the harvest festival.

Yellow – a host of spring daffodils
Mingling with the lush green grass;
The scene enhanced by the ceiling
Of a blue, blue sky.

There was indigo in the wings
Of a peacock butterfly
Flitting over the heath;
Whilst the modest violet nestled shyly
In the depths of the woodlands.

So the angel recycled the bow
Into a beautiful cloud:
A multi-coloured dream-cloud!

Champion Of Cheerfulness

I'm champion of cheerfulness
I'm cheerful every day
If others do not like it
Then let them go away!

I'm cheerful in the morning
I'm cheerful in the night
Who cares for moaning Minnies
Who wallow in their plight.

And even as I'm writing
I'm skipping to and fro
I'm moving like a dancer
Yarooh! I've stubbed my toe.

I'm moaning in my misery
'Cause I was having fun
I think I'll take an aspirin
My cheerful day is done!

Crazy Logic

Hey diddle dee, hey diddle dee
What are you doing there
Up in my tree?
With trousers all ragged
And torn to the knee
You're mad as a coot
Said I to he
So what are you doing there
Up in my tree?
Answer me please
By the count of three.

Well listen to me
Yes, listen to me
There is a good reason
I'm up in your tree.
I'm not on the moors
Nor walking the Lea
I'm not by the river
I'm not by the sea
I'm not on the bus
Or a train to Par-ee
But here I am sitting
Up high in your tree
Cos I had to be somewhere
Said he to me
I had to be somewhere, said he.

So confused by his logic I had to agree
And made him a nice cup of tea, of tea,
And made him a nice cup of tea.

Elders Of The Chapel

The Elders met one evening
Addressed by Brother Just
'I have a point I'd like to raise
How should we stand when giving praise?
As we are merely dust.'

So after much discussion
They declared and they beseeched
'I think it fair,' said Brother Grace
'We all take turns to state our case
So rulings can be reached.'

'I put my hands together,
When I pray,' said Brother Wright
'From infancy I learned the way
To say my prayers three times a day
By morning, noon and night.'

Said Brother Smith, 'That is a myth
The hands are used for labour
What counts is how you love your God
And how you treat your neighbour.'

'Now listen please,' said Brother Brown
'Prayers should be said when kneeling down
And even though we should be kneeling
Our hands should point up to the ceiling.'

Then up spoke Brother Jethro Fine
Who said, 'I pray when I recline
At night-time when I rest my head
I say my prayers upon my bed.'

Said Brother Good, 'When times are dire
Just be discreet like Nehemiah
Or spare a thought for Jeremiah
Who said his prayers down in the mire.'

The last word came from Brother Wise
Who said we ought to realise
That rather than debate or wrangle
We say our prayers from any angle.

Mutton-Glutton

A chap who was known as a glutton
Feasted all day on roast mutton
With a terrible boom
He blew up in his room
And all that was left was a button.

The Cycling Queen

One morning just by Worthing Pier
A hazy form was drawing near
And then a vision did appear –
A lady on a bike.

Her long skirt blowing in the breeze
Revealed a pair of shapely knees
She cycled by with silken ease –
The lady on the bike.

She wore a Mona Lisa smile
Exuding elegance and style
Compelling folk to look awhile –
At the lady on the bike.

I never met her face to face
As she went by at quite a pace
Such symmetry and feline grace –
The lady on the bike.

It's been a while since I have seen
The enigmatic cycling queen
Perhaps she's bought a limousine –
The lady on the bike.

Sign Of The Times

Before GPO was a force
Before man sent signals by morse
There were methods, no less,
Like the Pony Express
Where mail was delivered by horse.

Red Indians used to convey
Their thoughts in an unusual way
Smoke signals were sent
By the side of their tent
And always received the same day.

In Bible times runners were sent
Up hills and through valleys they went
In the cold and the heat
They relied on their feet
To relay every major event.

Today we are never alone
As long as we carry our phone
And let's not forget
By the use of the Net
We reach each terrestrial zone.

If you have a problem to share
There is One who is willing to care
It's a system Divine
With no telephone line
If you contact your Maker in prayer.

Birth Of Romance

From the clay of the Earth the Almighty
Formed the Father of all Humankind
To look after the Earth
From the time of his birth
And respect everything God designed.

God showed him the creatures in Eden
When Adam was all on his own
He noticed their state
That they each had a mate –
So why was he standing alone?

But God had a purpose for Adam
To father the whole human race
With miraculous power
He shaped in that hour
A woman of beauty and grace.

So theirs was the very first romance
When they were united as one
They bequeathed through their genes
The perpetual means
For true love that endures like the sun.

The Old Wurthytrudger

I'm one of the old wurthytrudgers
I keeps all the footpaths clear
So as folk can enjoy their rambling
Whatever the time of the year.

I do not get paid for my service
I works in the rain and the fog –
Just buy me a pint if you want to
I drink at the Shepherd and Dog.

I've risked all the wrath of the bullocks
When weather is making 'em prance
Cavorting and bucking like rabbits
They've led me a merry old dance.

I 'aven't been home for a fortnight
'tis said that I smell like a goat
Oh! How would you like a ripe pheasant?
I've got one just 'ere in me coat.

If you spot me when you are a'rovin'
And you've a cheese sandwich to spare
I'll save it for lunch with my cider –
That's what I call traveller's fare.

I sits on a log when I'm tired
Or a stile or whatever's near
I'm Simon the old wurthytrudger –
Just wave when you're passin' m' dear.

The Lurgashall Venture

We drove along the leafy lanes
Arrayed in all our finery
Then through the trees we saw a light
And found the Sussex Winery.

Into the ancient barn we strolled
And entered through the doors of bronze
Then all at once we saw a crowd –
A host of sparkling demijohns.

Beware the red stuff in the glass
The tot that has a cobra's bite
And shun the elderberry port
That leaves you senseless in the night.

Long time we sipped the mead and wine
Indulging in much repartee
Then in surprise Lord Jerry said
"Is that the time? Good gracious me!"

And so we made our journey home
Just floating o'er the Sussex Downs
All clutching trophies sealed with cork
For drinking in our nightie gowns.

With apologies to William Wordsworth and Lewis Carroll.

Sweetie

She announced herself in the Rue de Paris
A breathtaking model of sweet symmetry
The frilly skirt wafting just over her knees
Was teasing and tempting and fashioned to please.

Her roseate cheeks had the bloom of a peach
Like fruit in an orchard that's just out of reach
A vision in garments that floated so free
And cried out to onlookers – Hey! Look at me.

Attention! Attention she sought to invite
Alluring and tempting likc Turkish delight
Her lips, freshly plucked from a red-cherry tree
Seemed to give out a message – please come sample
me.

Like bright sugared almonds, oh! What a surprise
I looked and was hooked by her jewel-like eyes
That beautiful damsel, so moving to me
I saw from my wheelchair in the Rue de Paris.

The Missing Tarts

Our Bertie bought a vintage car
And drove it home with pride
Then Sister Susie said, 'Oh joy!
Please take us for a ride.'

So Mother said, 'Let's all go out,
A picnic I'll prepare.'
So off she went to bake some cakes
While Susie washed her hair.

Now Father liked to do his bit
So slipping on his shoes
He ambled to the Cock and Bull
To buy some cans of booze.

They made their way to Bognor beach
And picnicked near the sea
They laughed and joked beside the pier
One happy family.

And as the sun sunk slowly down
They clambered in the car
Then Bertie said, 'We'll soon be home
It isn't very far.'

The outing was a great success
Till trouble reared its head
'I fancy a jam tart,' said Mum
'Where have you put them Fred?'

They rummaged all around the car
Which made it shake and rock
And everyone was searching hard –
But Mother got the knock.

Said Mother, 'I've prepared the food
And really played my part
Now all I want for my dessert
Is just one little tart.'

'You never packed them I am sure,'
Dear Father dared to say
So Mother smacked him round the ear
And said, 'You'll rue this day.'

Now Dad was smarting from the blow
Which really shook him rigid
And on the journey back to base
The atmosphere was frigid.

Poor Father's face was full of fear
With Mother at his side
She turned her head and snarled at him
'I'll deal with you inside.'

Then Father stepped out from the car
And stooped to lace his shoe
When, to everyone's amazement
The tarts came into view.

Yes, there they were like traffic lights
Mother was in stitches
For all the time the tarts were there
Adhering to his breeches.

So as he wandered up the path
When day was nearly done
The jam tarts, ruffled by the wind
Just dropped off, one by one.

Now Mother couldn't get her breath
Her laughter was insane
So Father missed his telling off
And lived to fight again.

So take heed husbands, everywhere
Before the trouble starts
If you would like a quiet life
Don't mess around with tarts.

Flashy Fellow

There was a young fellow from Tring
Who kitted himself with cheap bling
A huge lightning strike
Blew him clean off his bike
And that was the end of his fling.

The Brighton Line

The South Downs, green from showers of rain
Seen from the Brighton line
Assure me that it won't be long
Before I'm home again.

The hills are getting closer now
The sheep are blobs of white
The iron wheels roll down the rails
As Sussex comes in sight.

We're travelling faster, faster still
The trees and fields a blur
There's Jack and Jill on Clayton Hill –
Then in through Brighton's door.

Straight through the belly of the downs
The mighty monster roars
On to the town where I was born
And where the seagull soars.

The brakes bite hard by Patcham Park:
The motors throb in time
I glimpse the Race Hill through the trees
And now I'm home again.

I've travelled up to John O' Groats
To France and Italy
But nowhere in the world compares
With Sussex by the Sea.